A Year of Mourning

A Year of Mourning

Poems 271–322 of
Petrarch's
Rerum vulgarium fragmenta

TRANSLATED BY
Lee Harlin Bahan

ABLE MUSE PRESS

Able Muse Press

www.ablemusepress.com

Printed in the United States of America

Library of Congress Control Number: 2017930344

ISBN 978-1-927409-95-4 (paperback)
ISBN 978-1-927409-94-7 (digital)

Cover image: "Out of Tune" quilt by Suzanne Marshall,
        photo by Charley Lynch and American Quilter's Society

Cover & book design by Alexander Pepple

Able Muse Press is an imprint of *Able Muse: A Review of Poetry, Prose & Art*—at www.ablemuse.com

Able Muse Press
467 Saratoga Avenue #602
San Jose, CA 95129

In Memory of Scotty Turley

Poem 271 begins a segment of 52 sonnets. The date I attach to 271 is January first, New Year's Day, and I would like to suggest that symbolically those 52 sonnets form *a year of mourning.*

—Thomas P. Roche, Jr.,
     "The Calendrical Structure of Petrarch's *Canzoniere*"

*O life of ours, looking to be so fair,
how cursorily you ruin in one morning
what a lot of years of great pain bought.*

—Francesco Petrarca,
     Rerum vulgarium fragmenta 269 (trans. L.H.B.)

*And that's what all the very greatest masters do. . . .
They make jokes.*

—Donna Tartt,
     The Goldfinch

Contents

Preface

FRANCESCO PETRARCA, PETRARCH TO ENGLISH SPEAKERS, 1304–1374, was the son of political refugees who fled Italy to settle near Avignon, France. Wanting to be a poet, Petrarch dropped out of law school when his father died, and returned to Avignon where, he claims, he fell in love at first sight of Laura, a married woman as God-fearing as she was beautiful, during Good Friday service in 1327. The event inspired a book called in Italian *Canzoniere,* "songbook," and *Rime sparse,* "rhymes spread (by word of mouth or in handwriting)."

Less well known is the work's official Latin title, *Rerum vulgarium fragmenta,* "partial text about common things." I prefer this title because its three words remind us that Latin was the language of Medieval high culture while the people of Italy spoke Italian in everyday life, and conjure sepia ink on scraps of discarded parchment showing that love and life's brevity are universal human concerns, and hint that the speaker has a thing for this lady so the subtext can get a little trashy. A web of such wordplay—studded with classical and Biblical allusions, and a cast of shifting images—holds together Petrarch's lyric account of unrequited love for a woman during her physical life and after she died of bubonic plague in 1348. In my opinion, *Rerum vulgarium fragmenta* fueled the Elizabethan literary achievement and informs Western popular song to this day.

Unsurprisingly, seven hundred years later, English translations of Petrarch abound; I have nineteen volumes of them. I feel more blessed than cursed to have come to this party late; every Petrarch translation I've read has taught me something or prompted my admiration in some way, so, the more the merrier. In fact, because plenty of scholarly and traditional translations privilege meanings that foreground the beautiful surfaces of Petrarch's work, I'm freer to privilege meanings that foreground an ugly form of *eros,* hoping that readers in a secular and sexually explicit age will take the speaker's struggle seriously, recalling that comedy is for those who think. Similarly, I doubt I do harm by clarifying a source poem's dramatic situation for readers who only have "seen" Black Death on *NCIS,* or, now that a basic liberal arts education is considered elitist, by supplying specifics of classical myths to which Petrarch alludes.

Thomas Roche, though, gave me the means to turn Petrarch from a building block of the ivory tower back into a bridge between classical and modern culture. Briefly, Roche relates the number of poems in *Rerum vulgarium fragmenta* to the number of days in a leap year, such as 2012, and relates poems 271–322 to the fifty-two days before Lent in that year, where *Rvf 271* represents January 1, as well as to the number of weeks in any year. What began as an experiment to test Roche's ideas, a cure for my desultory practice of translating Petrarch, yielded a free-standing sonnet sequence that can be pitched in one sentence: after a possible new love interest dies, the speaker revisits scenes from his relationship with the real love of his life, and, by mourning her untimely death, confronts his mortality.

While this excerpt panders to our twenty-first century attention span, we still are introduced to the Olympic gymnastics of Petrarch's thought uninterrupted—and performed to songs we know. Were Petrarch transported through time and space to the present day, and the pan-galactic language whatsit were working, he'd recognize the artistic ambition expressed in Pitchford's lyrics to "Fame." If you're familiar with the words to "Greensleeves," have heard Streisand performing "Evergreen," and America singing "Sister Goldenhair," you basically understand Petrarch's use of *lauro,* "laurel," a non-deciduous tree the leaves of which once crowned poet laureates, and of *l'auro,* "the gold," to play on Laura's name. Hammond's and Hazelwood's "The Air That I Breathe" addresses Petrarch's other essential pun, *l'aura,* "the air" or "the breeze." Come to think of it, since Jamestown was settled by people who could have seen premieres of Shakespeare's plays, and the KJV Bible followed in their wake, the distance from Petrarch to Butcher Holler to crying into beer in Nashville, or to Wonder's "You Are the Sunshine of My Life," isn't far.

Granted, politics as well as—the following is my guess—envy of Dante's acclaim motivated Petrarch to use the language of the common people of Italy as opposed to Latin, the common language of literate Medieval Europeans; World War II showed how ugly nationalism can be. In translating Petrarch into my idiolect born of forty years among rural Americans and two degrees at a local university, letting his argument in this idiolect, to paraphrase Emerson, warp the iambic pentameter template, and by hybridizing Dickinson's slant rhymes with the not at all ham-fisted rhyming of contemporary popular song lyrics, I've meant rather to illustrate the wisdom of Kelly's opossum, Pogo: "Yep, son, we have met the enemy and he is us." I use this quote not to advocate an intolerant return to full rhymes and strict meter, but to plead for inclusion and at least familial, if we can't manage divine, compassion for our flawed humanity.

In this same vein, when I adopted and adapted the editorial practice of adding italicized titles to Petrarch's poems, I told myself that I was eliminating the need for footnotes and other scholarly paraphernalia, having been taught in a graduate writing program to fear them almost more than abstractions; today when terms can be put in a search engine via technology from which most of us are inseparable, I might argue that I was saving myself time writing notes, and the world's trees. As I worked my way through *Rvf* 271-322, though, I noticed I was memorializing people I had lost—a neighbor, one of my husband's groomsmen—and wound up dedicating the whole shebang to my college roommate who was beautiful and made clover-chains for her hair and died young. Revising my three-year-old manuscript for publication, I see that I refer to popular culture, snatches of songs that were like wallpaper when I was growing up (and still Carpool Karaoke to), and to authors who have passed into high culture, for the same reason that Petrarch compiled the leaves of his book and searched Europe for, found, and shared classical works long lost, and the March Hare who became Old Possum wrote *The Waste Land*. I'm shoring things against my own ruin, and because you're reading this, and because I hope you'll look for personal and cultural cognates by which to understand Petrarch and other people of other places and times, they're shored against yours, too.

Lee Harlin Bahan

7 February 2017

A Year of Mourning

271: *Winded*

The blistering knot that held me while I tallied
hours for twenty-one whole years has given
way to Death, a heavyweight whose pull
I'd not encountered, nor do I believe

grief kills. Since my loss wasn't Love's desire,
he stretched a new snare in the grass, heaped
fresh kindling to start another fire,
and so had me at great pains to escape.

If I'd not experienced being out of breath
so much, I would've been picked up and burned,
particularly since I'm less green wood.

I have my liberty again—knot torn
in two, fire out, ashes spread—due to Death
against whom brawn and brains aren't any good.

272: *Bad trip*

Life runs away, not stopping for a break,
and Death pounds right behind like infantry,
and past and present things embattle me,
and eventualities also attack,

and memory and anticipation rock
my heart—up, down, back, forth—so, honestly,
if not for showing myself a little mercy,
I now would be past thoughts that make me ache.

If some place did my sad heart good, I head
there in my mind; then, on the other hand,
I see wild gusts put sailing on in doubt;

I see a storm in port, the pilot dead
on his feet, masts broken, fabric flapping, and
the pretty lights I used to make for, out.

273: *Madeleine, with a nod to Mortimer*

Poor soul, what's with all this retrospection,
when the good old days are irretrievable?
Where's the sense in providing fuel
to intensify self-immolation?

The soft words and sweet looks that, one by one,
you transcribed and depicted are celestial
now, and how delinquent and irrational
it is to look for them in this location

you well know. Don't bring what kills us to life
again, or pursue fuzzy, fallacious
arguments, but ones that point to a good end.

Pleased by nothing here, let's seek Heaven:
because we view that beauty dimly if,
living and dead, our peace is wrung from us.

274: *Jeremiah 17:9*

Peace, hard thoughts, please! Isn't it sufficient
that Love, Fortune, and Death beleaguer me,
stand at the gate, without my running into
more antagonists internally?

And are you, heart of mine, the same as ever,
subjecting just me to your treachery,
keeping barbarians under cover,
consorting with my fast, slick enemy?

You're where Love stashes surreptitious notes,
and where Fortune rolls out its pageantry,
and Death recalls the blow bound to turn my

remains to dust, and where my roving thoughts
get lies with which to arm themselves: that's why
I blame just you for all that's wrong with me.

275: *Shades of Orpheus, with a nod to Barnes*

My eyes, the light of our life has been eclipsed,
rather, has ascended to shine in Heaven:
we'll see her there yet, there she waits, and even,
considering our lateness, mourns perhaps.

My ears, angelic words come from her lips
in a place a better hearing is given.
My feet, the one by whom you used to be driven
exists outside the purview of your steps.

Why, then, are you all making war on me?
I didn't blind or deafen you; neither
did I trample hopes for her recovery.

Blame Death—rather, praise Him who frees and tethers,
shuts and opens simultaneously,
and after tears knows how to gladden others.

276: *Buboes*

Because abrupt departure from unhindered,
angelic apprehension of her has taken
my soul to quite a sad, stumped, horror-stricken
place, I attempt to put my pain in words.

Fit sorrow—surely!—leads me to lament:
Love and the one who caused it know my broken
heart lacks any other cure for sickening
details that occupy existence.

The one I couldn't handle, Death, you finished;
and where, Earth, glad a human face so fine
is yours now to keep secret, watch, and cherish,

does that leave me, disconsolate and blind,
since I don't have the sweet, romantic, unblemished
vision that induced my eyes to shine?

277: *2 Corinthians 4:8–9, KJV*

If Love conveys no thoughts outside the box,
I'll be hard-pressed not to abandon life:
remorse and terror give my spirit grief
because desire survives and hope was axed,

so that my life is totally perplexed,
despairing and in tears that won't shut off,
tired, rudderless, its course doubtful and seas rough,
without a standby sure to fix this fix.

A mental image leads me, since my true
guide rests beneath—*above* us, I should say,
and shines more powerfully than ever through

my heart, not eyes: sad flesh combats each ray
of light so very much looked forward to,
and has me going prematurely gray.

278: *Stop the tree, I want to get off*

In spring, when her beauty was in full bloom
and Love usually affects us most,
leaving her earthly covering in the dust,
my life's breath leapt for her eternal home,

alive and beautiful and bare—wherefrom
she masters me and saps my strength. Ah, final
day of life, why not scrape off this sinful
bark, and be my first in that to come,

since, as my thoughts pursue her straightaway,
my unimpeded soul would, too, and pass
gladly beyond where breathlessness dismays?

So there's poetic justice in delay's
ensuring I go down of my own ponderousness.
How fair death would've been three years ago today!

279: *Madonna*

If birds sing mournfully, or wind in summer
coaxes faint applause from emerald leaves,
or raucous, coruscating riffles murmur
beside this flowering, lush bank that gives

me somewhere cool to sit, consider love,
and write, I realize I see and hear her,
buried yet radiant and alive above,
providing all my sighs a distant answer.

"Why pine away before your time?" she says,
sorry about the state she's found me in,
"Pain needn't stream from your unhappy eyes

"for my sake. Day became unending when
I died. The instant my eyes seemed to close,
they opened to the light that shines within."

280: *Van Heusen and Cahn*

I haven't been where I could see so clearly
what I want to, now she's not to be
seen anymore, or where I felt so free,
or yowled until my passion filled the air,

nor have I seen a valley offering near
this many spots to sigh in privacy,
nor do I think Love had nests this pillowy
on Cyprus or any other shore.

The waters speak of love and breezes make
limbs quiver, and small birds, fish, flowers, and grass
implore as one I love and never stop.

But you remind me from the sky, born lucky,
how, before the time was ripe, you passed,
and pray that I'll look down on this world's pleasant traps.

281: *Eastwood*

How many times I head for my sweet refuge
to give others the slip (and me, too, were
it possible), the grass and my chest deluged
with tears, sighs shredding the misty air!

How many times, paranoid and alone,
I've gone to shady, obscure places where,
dredging my mind for sunken glints of the one
Death took, over and over I called her there!

Now looking like a nymph or other goddess,
she rises from the Sorgue's deep purity,
picks a spot on the bank, and takes a seat;

and then again I've seen her on spring grass,
crushing flowers as if with a living lady's weight,
regret showing on her face regarding me.

282: *Laredo*

Fortunate spirit who revisits often
to make torturous evenings comfortable
with eyes that Death not only didn't dull
but beautified beyond mortal fashion:

how over the moon I am to accept the vision
you permit, turning dark days wonderful!
So I begin detecting in their usual
haunts aspects of your loveliness again,

there, where I went around year after year,
singing about you. Now, as you see, my eyes
cry over you, no, not you, but pain I bear.

I find a respite just gasping for air,
so that, when you return, I recognize
your footfall, voice, face, and what sort of clothes you wear.

283: *Beast-whisperer*

You've drained the color, Death, from the fairest
face ever seen, and put the fairest eyes out,
and freed from that most elegant, fair knot
the soul in whom goodness burned with utmost

heat. In no time at all, you've dispossessed
me of my riches, stilled the most dulcet
tones ever heard, and made me mourn such that
no sight or sound attracts my interest.

My lady certainly returns to ease
much grief, wherever Pity has her go:
nothing else in this life relieves my cares.

And were I able to portray her glow,
mimic her speech, I wouldn't make love blaze
just in a man's heart, but a tiger's or a bear's.

284: *Harrowing*

The time and thought that resurrect my long-dead
lady vanish far too swiftly to
remedy my titanic suffering:
still, nothing does me harm while she's in view.

Love, having lashed and who nails me to this tree,
starts quaking when he sees her at my soul's
door, putting me out of my misery,
so quick and sweet-faced and soft-spoken still.

She comes as would a lady to her castle,
her smooth, bright forehead banishing sad notions
from a heart as down as it is dismal.

The soul, which can't bear such illumination,
sighs and says, "Oh, blessed hours of the day
when her eyes saw fit to open this passageway!"

285: *No-win*

A devout mother never gave her dearly
loved boy, nor passionate wife her cherished spouse,
sounder advice amid more numerous
sighs in a period of uncertainty

than she does me exiled in this sad place,
looking from Heaven's fastness, frequently
turning to me with her old warmth, pity
underlining her forehead's fairness twice:

now motherly, now like a lover, first
she's shy, then burns with righteous fire, and all
she says shows what on this journey to chase

or flee. Recounting our life, best to worst,
she prays I don't put off the uplift of my soul:
and only when she speaks do I have peace or truce.

286: *Miracles and Temptations*

If I could verbalize the delicate
breeze that I hear my former lady sigh,
who, though in Heaven now, appears nearby,
and lives, feels, takes walks, loves, and breathes, what heat

the words leaving my mouth would generate!
She comes back due to jealousy for my
soul and her piety, afraid that I
may tire, turn back, or stray from going straight

up as she teaches me to do; and, catching
pure enticements and reasonable pleas
sweetly murmured in compassionate, low tones,

I'm right with her, standing and on my knees,
since I pick up the softness in her speech,
whose virtue would squeeze tears out of a stone.

287: *Give my regards to*

Though you've left me to bear my pain alone,
Sennuccio, I still am comforted
again, because, transformed, head high, you've flown
from flesh in which you were cooped up and dead.

You now can see both of earth's poles at once,
the retrograde motion of the planets,
and how shortsighted people are, such that
my grief is tempered by your jubilance.

But I well may entreat you to salute
Guittone, Masters Cino and Dante,
our Franceschino—all that poetic host—

and tell my lady that tears constitute
a great part of my life, and I become a beast
recalling her fair face and deeds that were so saintly.

288: *Bad breath*

I've saturated the air hereabout
with sighs, looking from this difficult terrain
toward her birthplace on the yielding plain,
where, holding my heart, blooming and bearing fruit,

she went to Heaven, and, put in this spot
by her precipitous demise, my strained
eyes, failing at a distance once again
to glimpse her, dampen all that *is* in sight.

No stumps or boulders on these mountainsides,
no limbs or foliage along these banks,
no flowers in these valleys, no grass blades,

no droplets from these springs, no beasts that slink
beneath this forest's canopy are so uncouth
they don't know what a foul taste care left in my mouth.

289: *Castiglione*

Torch of my soul, the fairest of the fair,
whom Heaven showed friendship and courtesy
while here, has gone back, somewhat soon for me,
to her native country and deserving star.

Now I begin to wake and comprehend
that her sweet, stern face tempered my desire
and youthful lusts with which I was on fire,
for the better. I thank her for it and

for high-minded advice, that, with her looks
and gentle ridicule, made me think how
I might be saved from the fever in my blood.

Oh, subtle arts with apposite effects:
one works with words, the other quirks her brow.
I make her famous and she makes me good.

290: *Carrot*

Go figure! I'm delighted by and fond
of what displeased me most; I see and sense
that to get well I had to go through torment
and briefly fight for peace that doesn't end.

Oh hope, oh urge that always fools us, and
lovers more so by ten thousand percent!
Oh, how much worse if she'd made me content,
who sits in Heaven and lies underground!

But I was led so far astray by blind
Love and deaf intellect that they just up
and hustled me through life to Death's domain.

Bless her who willed I reach a better land
and turned my hellish wish into a fillip
to prevent my going down in flames.

291: *Zappa*

When Aurora comes down out of the sky,
with a blushing complexion and a golden mane,
Love hits me, so that I drain of color, sigh,
and say, "There—dawn and Laura now are the same.

"You're lucky, Tithonus, to know the time
of recovering your dear treasure well,
but what am I supposed to do now that I'm
obliged to die to see my sweet laurel?

"Your separations cause no difficulty:
at least she isn't put off by white hair
and shows up after her excursions nightly.

"But the one who took my thoughts into the air
with her darkened my days while evenings became
sad, and left me nothing except her name."

292: *Harrison*

The eyes of which I spoke so fervently,
along with the arms and hands and feet and face
that have cut me off to such a degree
from myself and the rest of the human race,

and her pure gold hair that shone and curled
and the lightning of her angelic smile that used
to make a paradise out of the world
are now a small, unfeeling pile of dust.

And I'm still here, which gives me pause and fits,
left without the light I adored so long,
on a boat with no mast in a mighty storm.

Let this be the coda of my loving song:
the source of my characteristic wit's
dry and my lute's in tune with those who mourn.

293: *Vale of*

Had I had any notion that the voices
of my sighs in rhyme would be so loved,
I'd have made more out of the ones I heaved
first, *in-* and *de*creasing their commonness.

With her deceased who caused me to express
myself, on whom I concentrate above
all, I can't, have no sweet file now to, give
my rough, impenetrable poems gloss.

My whole objective back then certainly
was getting melancholy off my chest
somehow, not pursuing celebrity.

I want to shed tears, not be honored for
them: much as I'd like to oblige now, her highness
calls me silent and exhausted after her.

294: *Matthew 5:15, among others, KJV*

As if she were a touring royal put
up until morning in a subject's shack,
she used to fill my heart with life and make
it beautiful: now her final step not

only rendered me mortal but has killed me,
and she's divine. My soul looted of all
its wealth, Love's lamp uncovered and the bushel
brought back down, should have rocks bursting with pity

but none can say how sad they are: their cries
echo inside where every ear is deaf
but mine, and I'm encumbered by such grief
that nothing lies ahead of me but sighs.

Truly, we're dust and darkness; truly, lust
is blind and greedy; truly, hope abuses trust.

295: *For Stephen McCauley*

My affections used to discuss their object
quietly among themselves: "She repents
her pity's coming late; maybe she mentions
us, hopes, or is apprehensive." Robbed

both *of* and *from* this life by her last instant,
looking from the sky's vault, she detects
and sympathizes with our predicament:
nothing else is left of her *to* expect.

O Gentile wonder, O glad soul, O rare,
superior beauty without precedent
or copy, here, then straightway gone home! There

a crown and palm attest her accomplishments,
which brought worldwide fame to, and made sense of,
her incorruptibility and my mad love.

296: *Chrétien de Troyes*

I used to fault and now pardon, i.e.,
applaud and love, myself for virtuous
incarceration, for the sweet, dolorous
blow I've borne many years in secrecy.

You snapped the spindle twisting a soft, shiny
strand into my life's thread, envious
Fates, *and* that rare, gold shaft that causes us
to like death better than is customary!

There never has been a soul that in its day
was so glad, free, alive, so addled
it wouldn't alter the instincts of its kind,

be cut so as to yelp for her always
instead of singing for another, thrilled
to die of such a wound and live in such a bind.

297: *Linnaeus, with thanks to Tedd*

Two mighty enemies came together,
Beauty and Noble Character, in such
peace that her saintly spirit wasn't touched
by rebellion after they moved in with her;

and now Death has sent them hither and thither:
the one is Heaven's glory, prompting much
pride there, while those fair eyes are cloaked from which
love-filled looks shot, and buried with the other.

Her kind deeds and wise, self-effacing words
that came from some deep place, and her heartrendingly
sweet glances that have left me scarred

are gone; and if I spend sufficient time
following her, perhaps, with this tired pen,
I'll set aside for God her lovely, genteel name.

298: *Romans 6:23, with a rhyme from Larkin*

When I look backwards at the years that have,
escaping, disseminated my ideas,
and quenched the conflagration in which I froze,
and terminated sigh-filled rest, and staved

in credence lent to lies told out of love,
and split my wealth, half going to the skies
and the remainder in the ground, and deprived
me of the compensation for malfeasance,

I snap out of it, and bare as Adam,
envy everyone about to pass,
and grieve, scared of committing suicide.

O Star of mine, O Luck, O Fate, O Grim
Reaper, O Day that to my mind is always nice
and mean, what a long way down you set me up to slide!

299: *Villon*

Where did the forehead go that with a slight
twitch sent my heart this way and that? Where are
the beautiful eyelashes and the stars
that gave the course of my existence light?

Where are her nerve and knowledge and insight?
Her canny, candid, plain, sweet banter?
Where are the beauties collected in her
that made their wishes my commands for quite

some time? What happened to fine shade cast by
a human face, refreshing my tired spirit
and that place where all my thoughts were penned?

Where is she who had my life in her hand?
What a huge loss this miserable planet
has suffered, and my eyes that never will be dry!

300: *McLean*

How jealous, greedy earth, I am of you,
embracing her I can't see any more,
keeping the beautiful face out of view
where I found peace in the middle of my war!

How envious of Paradise I am,
that palms and clenches and so lustfully
cloisters her spirit loosed from pretty limbs,
and all but never grants others entry!

How much I covet the predestined bliss
of souls at her holy and sweet side,
a place I sought with yearning all the time!

How greatly I begrudge that pitiless,
hard Death, having put out my life in her, abides
with those attractive eyes, and doesn't call me home!

301: *Longfellow*

Valley filled with echoes of my sorrow,
river that my tears are apt to deepen,
forest creatures, darting birds and minnows
bounced between this grassy bank and that one,

air steamed up and cleared by heavy sighing,
sweet path taken somewhere very bitter,
hill that pleased me and now has me dying
of regret, where Love leads me as ever:

plainly, your old features still are fresh, while
I'm less so; the prospect of such giddy
life makes me the home of endless grieving.

Here I saw my treasure; and from here I'll
walk back where her bare soul flew to Heaven
and this earth received the remnants of her beauty.

302: *John 9:4*

I rose in my imagination, where
the one I try but fail to locate here
was among those orbiting the sky's third tier,
and there I reenvisioned her: less proud, more fair.

Taking my hand, she told me, "In this sphere,
you'll be with me, if wanting that is right;
I'm the one who engaged you in all-out war,
and did my work before the coming night.

"My bliss can't be grasped by the human mind:
I only wait for you, and what you adored
and is below, my flesh's loveliness. . . ."

Why did she shut her mouth and drop my hand?
Because on hearing such pure, holy words
I hardly kept from staying in Paradise.

303: *Brothers Gibb via Hemingway*

Love, having stood beside me in fair weather,
between the Isle's banks, friendly to thoughts of ours,
and to bring our long-opposed camps together,
paced, reasoning with me and the Sorgue: flowers,

leaves, grass, shades, caves, riffles that the soft breeze stirs,
blocked valleys, steep hills, and rolling meadows,
the port of call of my romantic labors,
and heavy storms I often undergo.

O scampering woodland residents, O nymphs,
O fish suspended in and nourished by
these cool, sea-weedy, liquid crystal depths,

my once clear days now are as cloudy
as Death who made them that way! Just so, on earth
each person's destiny is fixed at birth.

304: *The one Paul Williams wrote for Karen and Richard*

So long as worms of love and flames consumed
my heart, hot on the faint, sporadic trail
of an undomesticated animal,
I searched the lonely, cloistered hills it roamed,

and dared complain, singing, about the trouble
Love caused me and the one I thought hide-bound,
but wit and poetry were thin on the ground
that season when my thoughts were fresh and unstable.

Beneath a bit of marble, that fire is dead,
which, had it grown, advancing with the decades
to old age, as in others has been the case,

armed with the rhymes that I put down today,
in geriatric style, would have me say
things to rend rocks and make them cry for sweetness.

305: *Numerous thanks to Marilyn Hacker*

Fair spirit freed from netting far more fair
than Nature ever knew how to design,
turn from Heaven, with my dark life in mind,
toward weeping after thoughts of rapture.

The heart's been disabused of that wrong notion
which sometimes made your sweet face hard and sour
to me: hereafter absolutely sure,
turn your eyes this way when I sigh, and listen.

Look *where the sheer gorge spreads its wooded thighs*
to bear the Sorgue and, between the grass and blue
flow, see one fed by memory and mourning.

I wish you'd leave the place your dwelling lies,
where our love sprang, to keep you from discerning
in what's yours that which displeases you.

306: *Habakkuk 3:19, for Billy Spray*

My sunshine, who disclosed to me the right
road on which to march to Glory, turning
to the Son of God, consigned my light
and her terrestrial prison to a cairn,

transforming me into a woodland beast
that sways on wayward, solitary feet
and with a heavy heart looks down through wet
eyes at a world which seems an alpine waste.

So I investigate every byway
where I saw her; and just Love, who inflicts
pain, comes to spur me on and show the way.

I don't find her, but see her holy tracks
all leading back toward the highest way,
a long way from avernal, stygian lakes.

307: *Or would you rather swing a birch?*

I thought myself dexterous enough to fly
(not under my own power, but through Him who
deploys my wings) by singing equal to
the pretty ties from which Death frees me and by

which Love binds me. In practice, I found I
was slower and shakier than a slight
limb bent by a considerable weight,
and said, "He aims to fall who jumps too high,

"and man can't do what Heaven doesn't approve."
No witty quill, much less a ponderous
style or tongue, could soar as Nature did making

my delicious stumbling block whom Love
proceeded to enhance with care so marvelous
I didn't deserve to see her: that was just my luck.

308: *Seger*

She's why I traded the Arno for the Sorgue
and fawning riches for frank poverty,
and who soured holy sweetness that sustained me,
leaving skin and bones fit for the morgue.

Since then I've tried and tried without success
to paint her high beauties in poetry
so she'll be cherished by posterity
but my style can't flesh out her lovely face.

Regarding good points only she possessed,
like stars that spread across the sky, from time
to time, I burn to outline one or two:

but when I reach the place where she's divine,
who was a brilliant, short-lived sun to humankind,
heat, wit, and art sail right on past.

309: *Pharos*

Love, who originally untied my tongue
so I'd reveal to those who weren't there what
they missed, turned quills, ink, paper, hours, and wit
to capturing a thousand times, all wrong,

the towering, new wonder that in our age was
put on earth and wished not to remain,
that Heaven let us peep at, then reclaimed
to illuminate its stellar passages.

My verses haven't reached their high point yet:
I know this in my heart, as anyone
does well who's talked or written of love to date.

Let the person who's imaginative
savor unsaid truth's victory over style, and then
sigh, "*That* was how blessed eyes were seeing her alive!"

310: *Liquefaction, and other allusions*

A vengeful wind restores fine days, bringing
its sweet kin up again, the hyacinths
and grass, and avian warbling and laments,
and the late, pure snow and squirming red of spring.

Beneath clearing skies, the meadows giggle,
and Jove brightens at Venus' appearance;
Love permeates the air, water, and soil,
and beasts without exception call for romance.

But I'm revisited by heavy sighs,
pulled from deep inside me by someone
who carried my heart's keys to Paradise;

and small birds making melody and budding
slopes, and in the modest undulations
of fair ladies, are waste land and wild things.

311: *Stones*

When out of tenderness that nightingale
fills sky and countryside with such a plethora
of wretched, piercing notes, bewailing
chicks perhaps or the consort of his youth

so delicately, and accompanies me the whole
night, I'm struck by my hard lot: in truth
no one's to blame but me because I failed
to see that goddesses were subject to Death.

How easy certain people are to trick!
Who knew two pretty eyes more luminous
than sunshine ever would turn this earth black?

I now know that my beastly luck's intent
is for long life and tears to get across
how nothing nice below is permanent.

312: *When deep purple fails*

Not by stars crossing skies without a cloud,
nor pitch-smeared carracks on quiescent seas,
nor countrysides kept safe by cavalries,
nor creatures glad to dart through a fair wood,

nor fresh news longed for when the old was good,
nor soaring, rich, romantic oratory,
nor sweetly singing, beautiful, real ladies
in green pastures where springs are free of mud,

nor by any other means can I be reached,
so deeply was my heart interred with one
who solely was my light and looking glass.

To live so long so gravely pains me such
that I beg for the end, desperate to see again
one I oughtn't to have looked at in the first place.

313: *Cash*

It's been a long time, sad to say, since I
lived with that much refreshment ringed by fire,
and she about whom I wept and wrote expired
but has left me a quill and tears to cry.

Her charming, saintly face is gone, but a look
in passing from those delicious eyes ran
the heart I used to own clean through, which then
went with her, enfolded in her lovely cloak.

She took it to the grave and Paradise
where she triumphs now, crowned with laurels
that the victory of her goodness merits.

If only I could shed the flesh my soul
wears, which detains me here, and be past sighs
in the company of beatific spirits!

314: *Body of work*

My mind, looking forward to your ruin,
already obsessed and sad in the good
old days, scrutinizing your beloved vision
to divine relieved breathlessness ahead,

clued by gestures, words, smiles, frowns, apparel,
and nascent compassion interspersed with tears,
you truly would've said, had you known all,
"Today is the end of my congenial years."

And how congenial, wretched soul, it was
to be incinerated by those eyes
I never would be pleased to meet again,

when I surrendered to them at departure,
as if asking that two faithful friends
attend a noble corpse, my cherished thoughts and heart!

315: *Checkered past*

Before all my flowering, green years were gone,
I felt the fire that seared my heart diminish,
and arrived at a place where life was one
long tumble downhill to the finish.

Prior to that my darling enemy
began to pluck up courage bit by bit
regarding her qualms, and made a game of it:
my bitter pain versus her sweet honesty.

The time was right around the corner where
Love is consummately chaste, and couples prize
sitting, and pull no punches when they share.

Death envied my euphoria, that is,
my hopes, and like an armed assailant,
jumped them on the way to their fulfillment.

316: *We're all the same height . . . in coffins*

The time was ripe for our great war's conclusion,
and peace or ceasefire might've come about
had the Great Equalizer of positions
not turned lighthearted steps into a rout:

because the one whose fair eyes guided me
was there, and then, like fog that whites things out
until the wind blows, wasn't suddenly,
these days we meet in my pursuant thoughts.

Lingering just a little, she'd have found
my altered hair and habits kept debates
with her about my failings well in bounds.

To what lengths, with what unadulterated
sighs, I'd have gone on about my hard work, which she
now surely sees from Heaven, and regrets with me.

317: *Walnetto, with a rhyme from Auslander*

Love had disclosed a quiet anchorage
in the storm's long darkness where I writhed
during the years I truly came of age,
which strips off vice, and virtue and honor clothe.

By then she'd have seen through my persiflage,
and my devotion wouldn't be a bother.
Ah, cruel Death, how quick you are to wither
fruit so slow to reach the juicy stage!

Were she living, we'd have arrived where I
would've spoken the antiquated load
of my delicious thoughts in her pure ears,

and maybe she'd have answered with a sigh
accompanied by some pious platitude,
our faces changed, and one another's hair.

318: *Genesis 5:24 and 2 Kings 2:11*

At the fall of something that reveals
itself, as if unearthed by spade or whirlwind,
spreading its noble leavings on the soil,
showing the sun dry twigs raking the ground,

I saw another that Love made my goal,
on which the muses had me write, that bound
my heart and lodged there, scaling trunk and wall
in ivy-fashion, up and all around.

That living laurel, where my soaring thoughts
and scalding sighs nested and never moved
the greenery of those lovely limbs a bit,

translated to celestial realms, left roots
in its true home, where the one calling in grave
tones still is, and the one responding, not.

319: *Be careful what you wish for*

My mind preserves my days, more light-footed
than deer, flighty as shadow, seeing so little
good that, had I blinked, I'd have missed it,
and some bittersweet hours that nothing clouded.

Miserable world, unstable *and* mule-headed,
the one who pins his hopes on you is really blind:
you're where my heart was taken and lies in a hand
the bones and nerves of which disintegrated.

But the perfected version of her that
still lives high in the sky, and will always,
makes me love her every beauty a lot

more and, just thinking what she is today,
and in what place she finally rests, and what
seeing her pretty flesh would be like, I go gray.

320: *All fall down, for Phil Andrews*

I feel yesterday's breeze, and see sweet hills
appearing where the lovely light was born
that caused, while Heaven pleased, my eyes to yearn
and be glad, but now, sadly, makes them spill.

Oh seasonal hopes, oh thoughts gone wild!
The grass is bereaved and the waters churn,
and the nest in which she lay is cold and barren,
where I lived anticipating burial,

aspiring, after many labors, to lie here
and rest a while among flowering bushes,
facing the bright eyes that set my heart on fire.

My master has been stingy, even vicious:
having burned as long as my flame was there,
I go around in tears now for spread ashes.

321: *Laura in disguise at sunset*

Is this my firebird's birthplace, where she decked
herself in gold and crimson plumes, and kept
my heart beneath her wings, and is adept
as ever at getting it to sigh and speak?

Oh, sweet rootstock from which I grew sick,
where has the face gone from whose good looks leapt
sparks keeping me on fire, alive and rapt?
Unique on earth, you rejoice with Heaven's flock.

And since you left me destitute and lonely,
sad to say, I always am returning
where I enshrine and bless your memory,

watching the shadows flicker, hills burning
black where you flew into eternity,
and once upon a time your eyes created morning.

322: *Auld lang syne—reply to the very bad poem of a long-dead, very good friend*

My dry eyes never are going to see
with my mind's dispassionate elements
those notes where Love's flame seems intermittent,
which might've been the workmanship of Pity.

Spirit not yet overcome through earthly
mourning, sufficient tenderness at present
drips from above to return my deviant
rhymes to that style from which mortality

estranged them: when my laurel crown was new,
I thought to show you other things my quill
produced. What cruel star envied us? Who too

soon took you, O my princely gem? Who conceals
you, seen with my heart, of whom I sing? And due to you,
sweet, great breath noisily relinquished, my soul stills.

Acknowledgments

I am grateful to Bruce Gentry and J.L. Kato, editors of print and online issues of *Flying Island* in which these translations originally appeared, sometimes in earlier versions: "279: *Madonna*," "299: *Villon*," "319: *Be careful what you wish for*," and "320: *All fall down, for Phil Andrews*."

Thank you to my teachers Willis Barnstone, Dick Davis, Robert Gross, Marilyn Hacker, Jeffrey Huntsman, and Maura Staunton; to my colleagues and friends Tony Barnstone, Pat Daily, Vince Gotera, R.S. Gwynn, Mark Jarman, Ruth Killion, J.D. Schraffenberger, and the *Eratosphere*'s online Translation Forum, circa 2006; to Suzanne Marshall, a photo of whose quilt greeted me on my computer's desktop and inspired me each day that I sat down to translate; to A.E. Stallings, from whom I'd rather have second place than a first from others; to Jeff Shutters, for taking author photos and providing jpegs on short notice; to Alex Pepple, for his editorial patience, perspicacity, promptness, and just plain helpfulness; and to my husband Pat, who tells me every morning to break a pencil and otherwise endeavors to be an angel in our house.

My claim regarding Petrarch's influence on literature and popular song first appeared in a biographical note that I wrote to accompany translations in *Natural Bridge*.

A grant from Driftwood Valley Arts Council (now Columbus Area Arts Council of Columbus, IN) enabled me to take Italian through the Division of Continuing Studies at Indiana University-Bloomington.

Mary Anderson Center for the Arts, Mt. St. Francis, IN, provided a residency during which I produced the draft that became "320: *All fall down, for Phil Andrews*."

The ninth line of "305: *Numerous thanks to Marilyn Hacker*" is paraphrased from Marilyn Hacker's "La Fontaine de Vaucluse" in *Taking Notice,* published by Alfred A. Knopf, 1980.

The twelfth line of "310: *Liquefaction, and other allusions*" contains my translation from *The Canterbury Tales,* "General Prologue," line 9, but reflects Petrarch's use of the infinitive.

"317: *Walnetto, with a rhyme from Auslander*" title derives from Walnettos, a caramel-walnut candy.

Works Consulted

Readers who want to check Petrarch's Italian can find *Rerum vulgarium fragmenta* online at www.italica.it/canzoniere.html or see Durling or Musa, listed below.

Armi, Anna Maria, trans. *Sonnets and Songs.* New York, NY: Pantheon, 1946.

Auslander, Joseph, trans. *The Sonnets of Petrarch.* London: Longmans, Green, 1932.

Bergin, Thomas, ed. and trans. *The Sonnets of Petrarch.* New York, NY: Heritage Press, 1966.

Bishop, Morris, trans. *Love Rimes of Petrarch.* Westport, CT: Greenwood Press, 1979.

Cook, James Wyatt, trans. *Petrarch's Songbook.* Binghamton, NY: Medieval and Renaissance Texts and Studies, 1995.

Durling, Robert M., ed. and trans. *Petrarch's Lyric Poems.* Cambridge, MA: Harvard University Press, 1976.

Hainsworth, Peter, ed. and trans. *The Essential Petrarch.* Indianapolis, IN: Hackett, 2010.

Juster, A.M., trans. *Longing for Laura.* Delhi, NY: Birch Brook Press, 2001.

Kilmer, Nicholas, trans. *Songs and Sonnets from Laura's Lifetime*. San Francisco, CA: North Point Press, 1981.

Kline, A.S., trans. *The Complete Canzoniere*. Poetry in Translation, 2001. Available online at www.poetryintranslation.com/PITBR/Italian/Petrarchhome.htm.

MacGregor, Robert M., trans. *Indian Leisure*. London: Smith, Elder, 1854.

Mortimer, Anthony, trans. *Canzoniere*. London: Penguin, 2002.

Musa, Mark, trans. *Petrarch: The Canzoniere*. Bloomington, IN: Indiana University Press, 1996.

Nichols, J.G., trans. *Canzoniere*. New York, NY: Routledge, 2002.

Roche, Thomas P., Jr. "The Calendrical Structure of Petrarch's *Canzoniere*," *Studies in Philology*, 71 (1974), 152-172. Ed. *Petrarch in English*. London: Penguin, 2005.

Shore, Marion, trans. *For Love of Laura: Poetry of Petrarch*. Fayetteville, AR: University of Arkansas Press, 1987.

Slavitt, David R., trans. *Petrarch: Sonnets and Shorter Poems*. Cambridge, MA: Harvard University Press, 2012.

Sonnets, Triumphs, and Other Poems of Petrarch: Now first completely translated into English verse by various hands, with a life of the poet by Thomas Campbell. London, Bohn, 1859. Available online at www.gutenberg.org/files/17650/17650-h/17650-h.htm.

Young, David, trans. *The Poetry of Petrarch*. New York, NY: Farrar, Strauss and Giroux, 2004.

Lee Harlin Bahan earned her MFA at Indiana University-Bloomington. Her thesis, *Migration Solo,* won the first Indiana Poetry Chapbook Contest and was published by the Writers' Center Press of Indianapolis. Her second chapbook, *Notes to Sing,* was recently published by Finishing Line Press. Lee's own poetry has appeared in *Ploughshares, The Kenyon Review,* and *The North American Review,* and her translations have appeared in *Natural Bridge, Southern Humanities Review,* and *Flying Island.* After receiving a local grant to study Italian, Lee enjoyed a month-long residency at Mary Anderson Center for the Arts, Mt. St. Francis, IN, pursuing her goal of translating Petrarch's sonnets. Lee read from *A Year of Mourning* at the University of Northern Iowa's *North American Review* Bicentennial Conference. The author lives with her husband Pat in a hundred-year-old farmhouse outside Medora, IN.

A Year of Mourning was a special honoree for the 2016 Able Muse Book Award.

photo by Jeff Shutters

ALSO FROM ABLE MUSE PRESS

William Baer, *Times Square and Other Stories*

Melissa Balmain, *Walking in on People – Poems*

Ben Berman, *Strange Borderlands – Poems*

Ben Berman, *Figuring in the Figure – Poems*

Michael Cantor, *Life in the Second Circle – Poems*

Catherine Chandler, *Lines of Flight – Poems*

William Conelly, *Uncontested Grounds – Poems*

Maryann Corbett, *Credo for the Checkout Line in Winter – Poems*

Maryann Corbett, *Street View – Poems*

John Philip Drury, *Sea Level Rising – Poems*

D.R. Goodman, *Greed: A Confession – Poems*

Margaret Ann Griffiths, *Grasshopper – The Poetry of M A Griffiths*

Katie Hartsock, *Bed of Impatiens – Poems*

Elise Hempel, *Second Rain – Poems*

Jan D. Hodge, *Taking Shape – carmina figurata*

Jan D. Hodge, *The Bard & Scheherazade Keep Company – Poems*

Ellen Kaufman, *House Music – Poems*

Carol Light, *Heaven from Steam – Poems*

April Lindner, *This Bed Our Bodies Shaped – Poems*

Martin McGovern, *Bad Fame – Poems*

Jeredith Merrin, *Cup – Poems*

Richard Newman, *All the Wasted Beauty of the World – Poems*

Alfred Nicol, *Animal Psalms – Poems*

Frank Osen, *Virtue, Big as Sin – Poems*

Alexander Pepple (Editor), *Able Muse Anthology*

Alexander Pepple (Editor), *Able Muse – a review of poetry, prose & art* (semiannual issues, Winter 2010 onward)

James Pollock, *Sailing to Babylon – Poems*

Aaron Poochigian, *The Cosmic Purr – Poems*

Aaron Poochigian, *Manhattanite – Poems*

John Ridland, *Sir Gawain and the Green Knight – Translation*

Stephen Scaer, *Pumpkin Chucking – Poems*

Hollis Seamon, *Corporeality – Stories*

Ed Shacklee, *The Blind Loon: A Bestiary*

Carrie Shipers, *Embarking on Catastrophe – Poems*

Matthew Buckley Smith, *Dirge for an Imaginary World – Poems*

Barbara Ellen Sorensen, *Compositions of the Dead Playing Flutes – Poems*

Wendy Videlock, *Slingshots and Love Plums – Poems*

Wendy Videlock, *The Dark Gnu and Other Poems*

Wendy Videlock, *Nevertheless – Poems*

Richard Wakefield, *A Vertical Mile – Poems*

Gail White, *Asperity Street – Poems*

Chelsea Woodard, *Vellum – Poems*

www.ablemusepress.com

www.ingramcontent.com/pod-product-compliance
Lightning Source LLC
Chambersburg PA
CBHW021510090426
42739CB00007B/550